NATIONAL GEOGRAPHIC

T0045235

# Round Like a Circle

Matthew Taylor

What is round like a circle?

An inner tube is.

What is round like a circle?

A Ferris wheel is.

What is round like a circle?

This highway is.

What is round like a circle?

This window is.

What is round like a circle?

A sunflower is.

# These are round like a circle.

Ferris wheel

highway

inner tube

sunflower

window